# Mother to Son

# Mother to Son

Shared Wisdom
from the Heart

Melissa Harrison &
Harry H. Harrison Jr.

WORKMAN PUBLISHING COMPANY • NEW YORK

Library of Congress Cataloging-in-Publication Data

Harrison, Melissa, 1951-
  Mother to son : shared wisdom from the heart / by Melissa Harrison and
Harry H. Harrison Jr.
    p. cm.
  ISBN 978-0-7611-7486-8 (alk. paper)
1. Mothers and sons--Miscellanea.  I. Harrison, Harry H. II. Title.
HQ755.85.H3746 2013
649'.132--dc23

                                                        2012034400

Design by Janet Vicario

Workman books are available at special discounts when purchased in bulk
for premiums and sales promotions as well as for fund-raising or educational
use. Special editions or book excerpts can be created to specification. For
details, contact the Special Sales Director at the address below or send an
email to specialmarkets@workman.com.

Workman Publishing Company, Inc.
225 Varick St.
New York, NY 10014-4381
workman.com
fearlessparenting.com

WORKMAN is a registered trademark
of Workman Publishing Co., Inc.

Printed in the U.S.A.
First printing March 2013
10 9 8 7 6 5 4 3

# Acknowledgments

This book was twenty-six years in the making and is the product of the wisdom of many outstanding moms. Charlotte Lee and Judy Birkes offered valuable insight.

# Preface

*"As a mother, my job is to take care of what is possible and trust God with the impossible."*
—Ruth Bell Graham

*"It's a boy."*

With these words, each mother starts a journey. This book is a guide to navigating the relationship—sometimes exhilarating, sometimes exasperating, but always extraordinary—between a mother and her son. The wisdom on these pages is intended to make you laugh, to make you sigh, and to give you strength. It's not easy to raise a loving, strong, and successful boy, but with each milestone—from the first bedtime story to the last day of school—you'll be reminded that you're doing the most important job in the world.

# The Five Keys

### 1.
Pray for him every day.

### 2.
Respect his father.

### 3.
Do everything in your power
to create a peaceful home.

### 4.
Feed him love, morals, values,
and integrity daily.

### 5.
Be a strong woman.

# In the Beginning

Realize that your son will love you more intensely than anyone or anything else in the world.

At times, you will be blown away by the depth of your love for him.

Don't forget that as a baby, he will always be looking for your face. It will be this way forever.

Spend as much time with him as you can. This is for your sake as well as his.

Read all the advice
books and baby guides
you want, but trust
your instincts.
They're good.

Watch out when
you're changing
his diaper. Baby boys
shoot straight in
the air.

Know that your job in life is to feed him, love him, and point him in the right direction.

Be ready for him
to wake up hungry.
Boys eat more than
you can imagine,
even as babies.

Keep lots of
soft towels handy.
He's a drooling
machine.

The more you talk to him, the sooner he'll talk to you.

Don't speak to him
all the time in
baby talk.

Realize that from day one, he's wired to be self-reliant. Don't change that.

If you wait until he
cries to pick him up,
you're teaching
him to cry.

He will need a nap
every day for his
first five years.
So will you.

Accept the fact that boys and girls are different.

Steel yourself for when the doctor has to give him shots. His screams will wake the dead.

Baby-proof your home. Anything he can reach, he will put in his mouth.

You'll come to
appreciate baby
shampoo as one of
the world's greatest
inventions.

You will want to
just watch him—
his eyes, his hands,
his movements—
for hours. It's normal.

Remember,
he needs to be
around you,
to hear your voice,
to see you looking
at him.

# Relax.
# Throwing food
# is normal.
# Heck, throw it back.

Driving in a car
will put him to sleep.
Keep this in mind
when it's two a.m. and
he won't stop wailing.

Take him for walks.
Tell him what
he's seeing.

You don't have to be a constant source of entertainment. Let him entertain himself. Everything is stimulating to babies.

Buy him a soft blanket. He will keep it for years.

Keep in mind that
from the moment he
starts crawling,
he's tasted freedom.

Don't worry about falling off your exercise program. Once he starts walking, chasing after him will more than make up for it.

# Set up a college savings plan.
# Now.

You'll remember his laughter at this age forever.

Don't forget,
he needs one-on-
one attention
from you.

Practice staying calm.
This will serve you well
in his teenage years.

For reasons unknown,
he will want to sit in
your closet and play
with your shoes.
For hours.

Don't freak out when his dad throws him up in the air while playing with him. They both need this.

For a while—a long while—he will regard his father as more fun than you. But he will always know who feeds him and comforts him. Always.

It's okay if he
falls down.
What's important
is that he learns
to pick himself up.

# The Toddler Years

Note that his idols
will always be boys five
years older than he is.

You'll be tempted to throw elaborate birthday parties for him, even when he's one or two or three. You may love it, but at this age, he won't even remember.

Be consistent:
with your love, with rules,
with discipline.
With everything.

# Try to make rules fun.

His tears will
break your heart.
So will his smiles.

Remember, boys tend
to be competitive
about everything.
It will make no sense
to you and sometimes
scare you to death.

Don't panic over his eating a bug or two. Boys just want to know what things taste like.

Tell him to aim when
he uses the bathroom.
Until he does,
he will hit everything
*but* the toilet.

Remember,
toddler boys
are terrors. It goes
with the age.

He will be itching
to go outside
all the time.
Take him out.

If you make
fun of him,
he'll learn to
be shy.

# Don't overreact when he hurts himself, and he won't, either.

Try as you might,
you can't shield him
from life.

The sooner
he learns to
follow the rules,
the easier
his life will be.
And yours.

He will become unraveled when you leave him with a babysitter.
Go quickly.

Introduce him to crayons and paint. But keep an eye on him or he'll redecorate your home.

Install safety locks
on all the cabinets
he can reach.
This is as much
for your sanity as
for his safety.

Right around the
age of three,
he will heroically
start to think he is
your protector.
This never goes away.

If you want him to listen to you when he's a teenager, teach him to listen to you now.

Nightmares can terrify him. Hold him, comfort him, and watch over him until he falls back to sleep. In *his* bed.

He'll continue to
whine for as long
as it works.

From you, he'll learn the importance of telling the truth. Be a good model.

Remember
these words:
*It's just a phase.*

Make him drink
his milk. But don't
make him clean
his plate.

Don't skip nap time, or you will both pay dearly.

If you buy him
something every
time he goes to the
store with you, you'll
soon be buying him
something every time
he goes to the store
with you.

Establish a daily time
for reading together,
and stick to it.

No one has ever figured out how bubble gum winds up in boys' hair.

Don't install white carpeting. You're just inviting misery.

Enjoy his bath time.
He certainly will.

Tell him your kisses magically heal skinned knees. Distribute magic kisses liberally.

Teach him how to make a peanut butter and jelly sandwich. This could be his main source of sustenance for the next ten years of his life.

Don't forget:
Praise is contagious.
So is criticism.

Play catch with him.
He won't really care if
you can't catch a ball
or throw a perfect pass.

Remember, your encouragement breeds confidence. It always will.

To a young boy,
happiness is a big
spoon and a bowl
of chocolate chip
cookie dough.

Teach him to talk with
his mouth open and
chew with it closed.

He will try to drag a hose from the backyard into the living room. Discourage this.

He will continually be fascinated by things he finds in his body.

Gently remind him that anything he finds in his nose should, for the good of society, stay there.

Teach him to
check his zipper.

He will want a bike.
He will fall off it.
He will live.

Your purse will always be a source of mystery to him.

Take walks with him at his pace. He could spend five minutes watching a doodlebug.

Show him how to fold his clothes. But don't expect miracles.

# Teach him manners.

Let him teach you how to skip stones.

Learn to
make a good
explosion noise.
He'll think you're
amazingly cool.

Don't let his father forget that his son is still a little boy.

# Don't tolerate his tantrums. Ever.

He will always want to show off his injuries. Act horrified.

Try not to spend
time arguing.
Make a decision
and move on.

No matter how
much he protests,
put him in his car seat.
In the backseat.

Be prepared when taking him shoe shopping. Boys test new shoes by racing down the aisles of the shoe store.

At a certain point in time, he will think peeing is the most fun you can possibly have in life. He'll move on.

Teach him to help you out around the house. He'll be more useful later, when he's a teenager.

If he comes home
filthy and muddy,
have no qualms about
hosing him off before
letting him back inside.

Take him to the store
with you. Let him
pick out the juice,
the apples, the cereal.

He will delight in grossing you out.

Show interest when he brings home yucky stuff. The more scared you act at the sight of the worm, frog, or cricket, the happier he'll be.

Teach him how to set the table. This will amaze future girlfriends.

Let him be a boy. Don't expect a "little gentleman" at age five.

When all else
fails, give him
cookies and milk.

# Sports

Put your fears aside. Even if he's small and slow, he needs to play.

Always be his
cheerleader.

For many years,
it won't matter to him
if he wins, only that
he's playing.

Give him swimming lessons early. Waterproof him as a baby.

Generally speaking, your advice in picking out soccer or baseball shoes is not welcome.

Be prepared:
The price of his athletic
equipment will make
you consider taking
out a second mortgage.

He'll always look for you at his games. Sit where he can see you.

It's okay if you don't love attending his meets. But it's important that you're there cheering when something exciting happens.

Remember,
even perfectly
sane moms tend
to freak out during
soccer tryouts.

If he gets cut from a team, it will be one of the worst days of his life. And yours.

You will realize early on that there are two kinds of moms: those who coach, and those who never trust their sons' coaches.

If he's old enough to play, he's old enough to carry his own equipment.

Be prepared:
Even five-year-old
boys knock each
other down, fight,
and get emotional
during games.
Boys are like that.

Don't become the mother lion when another boy bulldozes him. It's all part of the game.

He won't understand
if you cry just
because he's bleeding.
Because his friends
will think the blood
is cool.

Tell him he had a great game, even if there's overwhelming evidence to the contrary. He just needs to hear you say it.

Keep sports fun for
as long as possible.
Remind his dad of this.

# Grade School

Walk him to school
for as long as he'll
let you.

Give him piano lessons—he'll thank you for them when he's older. But if you're constantly yelling at him to practice, something is wrong. With you.

Remind him that passing gas is hysterically funny only to other boys.

Expect roughhousing. It's loud, but it's normal.

Remember,
boys show their
affection by wrestling,
pushing, and bumping
into one another.

Don't go nuts
if he messes up.
He's still just a
little boy.

Teach him to
be kind.

Teach him the right
way to use mouthwash,
or else he'll swallow it.

Remember, he's probably hungry. Even if he just ate.

Teach him to
hang up his clothes,
even if it's easier to
just pick them
up yourself.

Don't worry about spending quality time with your son. Just spend *time* with him.

Remember,
the greatest gift you
can give him is the
strength to solve his
own problems.

Buy him a chemistry set and help him make something with it. *Ooh* and *aah* over how dangerous it is.

Boys love toy cars.
It's inexplicable.

Don't focus on turning
him into a man.
But don't let him stay
a little boy.

When he
dresses himself,
tell him he looks great.
Don't worry about
what others might
think.

Always, always, always know what he is watching on TV or doing on the computer.

Firmly establish the ground rules about his grades. Make sure he knows that they are the number one priority.

Get to know
his teachers.
They now spend as
much time with him
as you do.

Don't miss his school plays. Even if his role is Tree #2.

Every once in a while, eat lunch with him at school. Find out what's going on in his world.

Realize that he will always come to you for a yes after Dad says no. Because you're a soft touch.

His spontaneous hugs might stop when he's around eight years old, but don't worry— they'll be back.

As wild as
they might be,
little boys need
hugs for security.
So do big ones.

When you're at the store together, teach him about money. Explain that some things are too expensive.

Talk to him about saving for the future. Give him a piggy bank.

Picking up after him all the time doesn't show how much you love him. It shows how much he can manipulate you.

Teach him to wipe his
mouth on a napkin,
not on his shirt.

He will want
a puppy.
He will love it.
You will clean
up after it.

Resolve to spend
an hour every day
just having fun
with him.

# He will idolize
# his dad.

He will want you
to feel his muscles.
Tell him he's
a hunk.

Join the PTA.
Volunteer as
a classroom aide.
Know what's going
on at his school.

Remind him that every single action—good or bad—has a consequence.

Check his backpack nightly. He will let important information die in there.

Don't try to make
him into the man you
always wanted.

Teach him to read the instructions. His dad might have missed this.

Have tea with him
in the afternoons.
Serve cookies.

Remember, well-adjusted boys have loving mothers who are a source of strength, not criticism.

Watch your behavior around him: your language, your mores, your alcohol intake. He's watching you, and learning.

Show him how to hold a baby.

Avoid telling him to walk or talk "normal." Let him be himself.

The time to shape his behavior isn't during high school, but grade school. By high school his morals and values are firmly established.

Let him grow up.

The longer you
baby him,
the longer he'll
stay a baby.

Don't get in the habit
of making excuses for
him, or you'll be doing
it for the rest of his life.

Give him a Valentine's Day card every year. He'll say it's corny, but secretly he'll always look forward to it.

He will always
look to you
for love.

Teach him how to use the microwave—without blowing up the kitchen.

Never call him
names.

You will always
feel his pain.
But don't mistake
it for your own.

Don't get in the
habit of offering him
anything in the world
to make him happy,
or nothing in the
world will.

If he's being picked on
in school, it's important
he solve the problem
himself. Advise, but don't
interfere. It will just
humiliate him and make
matters worse.

If there's no one around to teach him how to defend himself, send him to karate lessons.

If you discover that *he's* the bully, realize something is very wrong. Usually at home.

Talk to him about sex and drugs and alcohol and parties, even if you think he's too young. Middle school awaits.

Surprise him by taking
him out of school and
bringing him to
a baseball game.
He'll never forget it.

# Spirituality

Talk to him often about God's grace and he'll grow up seeing it.

Little boys love to bang their feet against the pews during church services. Remove his shoes and he'll sit a lot more quietly.

Teach him his prayers.
Say them with him
every night as a family.

Buy him a children's bible and read it with him.

Treat his father
with love and respect.
Show your son that
being a man is a
good thing.

One way to get him to go to church services peacefully is to let him bring his friends along.

# Don't tolerate meanness.

Be consistent
with worship.
Go regularly.

Have him join a youth group. He'll like it more than he'll expect to.

Teach him to start an active prayer life *before* he's taking an exam he hasn't studied for.

Don't let him beg off attending worship or religious school. His time there will pay huge dividends down the line.

Say a blessing at every meal. Remind him that even the food he eats is a gift.

Stand up for your
morals. Don't give in.
He might protest now,
but eventually he
will model himself
after you.

Don't forget that although an active spiritual life doesn't solve all of life's ills, it does prevent quite a few.

Even when he's older, remind him to say his prayers.

Make sure his home
is a haven of love
and peace.

Don't forget that
God has given
you an awesome
responsibility:
raising a son in
today's world.

# Middle School

# Remember,
# all boys rebel.

# Demand respect.
# At all times.

Keep in mind that he's
not a child anymore,
nor is he an adult.
Treating him like
either one will lead
to disaster.

Keep kissing him good night. Even if he doesn't kiss back.

The single best way
to avoid turbulence in
his teenage years
is to surround him
with love, stability,
and family in his
formative years.

Don't shield him from
the consequences
of his bad behavior.
Dealing with the
aftermath of his
actions will make him
a better person.

If he's caught cheating at school, don't yell at the teacher. Lower the boom on him.

Ask him who the vice president of the United States is. Make sure he knows about the world he lives in.

Look him in the eye and tell him that if he ever starts doing drugs, life as he knows it will come to an end.

If he's getting in trouble at school all the time, it probably *is* his fault.

Prepare to spend the
next few years in
the car, driving him
and his friends around.

Play Beethoven
in the mornings.
It will calm
everybody down.

State, in your harshest mother-voice, that under no circumstances, in this lifetime, may he jump off any roof into a pool.

Know that left unattended for one second, however, he *will* jump off the nearest roof into the nearest pool.

It's hard for some moms to establish rules and stick to punishments for breaking those rules. Especially if there's no man around. But you must.

Don't be upset that you can't afford everything he wants. A small country couldn't even afford everything he wants.

Don't negotiate the punishments for his wrongdoings *after* he's been caught.

Tell him that studying hard and respecting his teachers' authority are crucial to avoiding problems in school.

Teach him that trust is something that can be lost in the blink of a lie.

Remember,
success breeds
success.

He will want you to be his friend. But what he really needs is a mom.

Everything will
smell better when he
starts using soap.
And deodorant.
Regularly.

Be assured that fathers have been left alone with their sons for eons, and the human race has continued.

Talk to him.
Ask questions.
All the time.
Let him know you're
aware of his life.

If you don't teach him
to do his laundry,
you'll be doing it
for him for as long
as he lives with you.
And probably after.

Remind him not to mix whites with colors unless he wants to wear pink socks to gym class.

Remember: Kids who aren't involved in any activities hate middle school. Kids who join extracurricular activities make tons of friends. And love middle school.

Do not let one
single disrespectful
comment slide.
Ever.

He's ready to learn about girls. He can either learn the facts from you, or get complete fiction from his friends and MTV.

Remind yourself that when he doesn't want to talk to you about something, that's when he most needs to.

He'll never stay
mad at you.
You're his mom.

Eat dinner as a family as often as possible. Talk about politics, the economy, sports, art—anything engaging. You will grow together.

Remember,
boys need fathers
to learn how to
become men.
He needs to spend
time with his dad.

Tell him how he can
earn your respect:
by speaking the truth,
keeping his grades up,
treating family members
with kindness, doing his
chores, and seeking to
serve others.

Be a part of his world. Know what games he plays, what shows he watches, what music he's listening to, who his friends are.

Ask yourself:
Do you care enough
about his growth to
*not* let him play violent
video games?
Don't give in just so
you don't have to listen
to his whining.

Boys this age will generally try out rude behavior on their moms that they wouldn't dare try on their dads. Don't allow it.

Tell his dad that it's
time for him to talk
with his son about
sex. Understand that
neither will be crazy
about the idea.

Don't let him
make fun of other
people.

Make sure he does volunteer work. It's a proven way to prevent him from thinking only about himself.

Never let him get the idea that he's the boss.

Teach him how to sew on a button.

Don't miss attending
a performance or
a game that he's
involved in.

Make sure he knows
that boys can do
anything girls can do.

Remember, your job isn't to do everything for him. It's to teach him how to do things for himself.

Teach him never to
be satisfied with the
status quo.

If his grades slip,
make him study
in front of you,
at the kitchen table.
His grades will improve
dramatically.

Remember, it's *his* homework. Check to make sure he's done it, but don't do it for him.

Don't judge his fun by what appeals to you. Most boys are more aggressive and thrill-seeking than their moms are.

If you don't believe
in him, it will be hard
for him to believe in
himself.

Feed his friends. You'll learn about them—and your son—as they raid the fridge.

Be unified with
his father.

Keep in mind that he's listening to every word you say. Especially when you say something negative.

Don't ask his teachers for special favors. They'll think of your son as someone whose mom is looking after him. That kind of reputation will follow him for years.

Be strong. This is not the time in his life to relax the rules.

If he complains that other kids get a bigger allowance or more things, don't give in. He'll live.

Show him how to boil water. He thinks he knows how. He doesn't.

Buy him food he
can make himself:
sandwich stuff,
oatmeal, canned soup.

Make sure he eats his spinach. And anything else you cook for him.

Don't let him hurry through dinner and leave once he's finished. Have him sit at the table until everyone else is done, too. Then have him help clean up.

Know that the longer he spends styling his hair, the goofier it will look.

He will start using
copious amounts
of cologne.
You might have to
stagger outside for air.

When planning a family vacation, think ski slopes and beaches instead of museums and sightseeing. Boys are restless.

Don't forget, he needs to know you're always there. No matter how weird he gets.

Remember, he's always testing the boundaries. Think long and hard before letting them move so much as an inch.

Every now and then
go into his room,
sit down, and just visit.

Insist that he let you know where he is at all times.

One of the great things about having a thirteen-year-old boy is that he can program the remote control, debug a computer, and load music onto your iPod.

Encourage him to read: sports pages, skateboarding magazines, Shakespeare—as long as he's reading.

Remember, in middle school you can forbid unsafe peers in his life. In high school, you can only forbid them in your house.

Tell yourself,
"He's not angry,
he's not an alien,
he's not mental.
He's just thirteen."

# Girls

If he becomes paralyzed when a girl says hello, you'll know he's discovered the opposite sex.

Don't push him into a romantic relationship. Not now. Not ten years from now. Not ever.

If he starts calling girls derogatory names he's heard on his iPod, it's time for a stern heart-to-heart. And lose the iPod.

Inevitably,
a girl will break
his heart.

He might start
middle school
a good foot shorter
than most girls.
Don't worry.
He'll grow.

Remember,
boys show affection for
girls by teasing them,
wrestling with them,
and generally annoying
them. Girls somehow
get the message
anyway.

Keep in mind that in adolescence, his being able to say that he has a girlfriend is more important than the actual girlfriend.

Don't let him
spend every dime
he's earned on her.

He will need you to explain the way girls think. His dad can't help him here.

Don't even think of
sending him to a party
without knowing
who will be there and
making sure that the
host's parents will
be home.

You can't stop him from falling for a girl whose life is in chaos. But you can explain what her life could do to his.

Television and the Internet are teaching him that women are promiscuous and shallow, and only want to date rock stars. He needs you to correct this impression.

Be careful not
to attach special
meaning to any of his
girlfriends. They will
come and go.

Remind him to buy his prom date a corsage. Remind him several times.

Don't be surprised when the girl he introduces as his future wife is uncannily similar to you.

# High School

Believe in him.
More than he
believes in himself.

Remember,
you'll always be one
of his most important
role models.

Praise him
not only for his
accomplishments
but also for the
quality of his
character.

Try to see
things from his
point of view.
Sometimes.

Don't forget:
A teenage boy's
brain is an
unfathomable thing.

Make sure he knows
that his grades matter
more than ever now.

Tell him often what
it is you respect
about him.

Find out what
motivates him,
what inspires him,
what fires him up.

Accept the fact that he'll be in a bad mood for the next four years.

Don't expect all his actions to make sense. In many ways, he's still a child.

If he knows he can come to you with a problem, he will.

Appreciate his accomplishments. Your opinion means everything to him.

Learn the difference between supporting him and rescuing him.

Hold him
accountable for
his actions.

He will always need you when he is in pain—emotionally, spiritually, or physically. Always.

If he loses
your trust,
let him earn it
again.

Expect success.
Expectations have
a way of becoming
reality.

Don't be the "cool mom" who permits underage drinking. You're sending him the message that it's okay to break the law—and that you don't care if he does.

Don't be quick to give him cash every time he asks for it. You're teaching him to rely on you for money instead of earning it himself.

Don't feel sorry
for him.
That doesn't
do him any
long-term favors.

Remember,
he will resist
maturity for as
long as you
let him.

If you have
a fixation on
brands and labels,
he will, too.

Don't be concerned with him disliking you. Instead, be concerned with him respecting you.

He will be capable of eating a huge dinner, going out with his buddies, and—an hour later—eating dinner again. It's normal.

To your amazement,
he will want clothes
that cost more than his
dad's do. This is when
you sit him down and
explain the concept of
getting a job.

Don't let him tell you
that he doesn't have
time for a job.
He has time.

Remind yourself
that you can't buy
his love.

Remember, he's a boy.
He thinks differently
than you. Before
you decide he's the
weirdest person on
the planet, check with
his dad.

# If you're criticizing him constantly, the problem is you.

Remember,
low grades are one of
the first indicators that
something is wrong.

Make him talk to you.
Don't let him shut you
out of his life.

He will want to talk
at the oddest,
most mysterious,
most inconvenient
times. Stop what you're
doing and talk.

Realize that his friends are vitally important to him right now. Condemning them will only alienate him from you.

When he first gets his driver's license, he *will* get lost. Make sure he has a cell phone. Or a smartphone with GPS.

When he's driving and you're in the passenger seat, don't scream, have a panic attack, or claim he's trying to kill you. Be calm. Be calm.

He doesn't need
a radar detector.
If he's getting
speeding tickets,
he needs to slow down.

If he does get a ticket, don't try to get it fixed. Send him to court. Wearing a tie.

Keep him busy outside of school—with reading, sports, clubs, lessons, a job. It means he has less time to find ways to get into trouble.

Take him to
the theater.
Have him drive.

Remind him to smile.

Talk to his friends'
parents. Find out
what's going on
over there.

Remember,
if he smells odd to you,
he smells odd to
the world.

There will come a
time when he'll try
to influence your
wardrobe choices.
Ignore him.

Don't hold him back. Let him be independent.

Make sure he knows that who he can be doesn't depend on who he has been.

If it's dangerous,
life-threatening,
and makes no sense,
he will love it.
Brace yourself.

# Don't defend his mistakes.

Insist he pick up after himself. Don't tolerate him being a slob.

Tell him you're
proud of him.
Tell him why.

Never treat him like
your parent, husband,
or best friend.
He's your son.

Never allow his emotions to rule the house.

Talk about the future.
Find out what he sees
himself doing with
his life.

Even throughout college, he will think money grows on trees. Correct his thinking.

Never buy the argument that none of his friends have curfews.

Learn to listen without judgment. Or even talking.

Don't take everything he says to heart. Boys like to try out ideas on their moms, then merrily go out and horse around while their mothers lie in shock on their beds.

Teach him to write thank-you notes. It will serve him for the rest of his life.

He will spend hours
obsessing over cars you
will never buy for him.
It's a guy thing.

Remind him that
each time he loses his
integrity, it becomes
harder and harder
to get it back.

Apologize to him
when you screw up.

Teach him that sharing what he has is one of the keys to happiness.

Don't simply criticize what's on TV. Unplug the set.

Realize he may choose a college because it:

a) is known as a great party school

b) attracts the best-looking women

c) has a beach nearby

Help him get his priorities straight.

Your heart will break whenever he's unhappy. This will be true pretty much forever.

His weekend nights might start later, but the curfew still applies.

Insist he watch
his language
around you.

Fix him snacks when he's up late studying. It will help keep him going.

Remember,
the stronger a mother
you are, the stronger a
man he will become.

Refuse to feed him until he completes his college applications. That will motivate him.

# Leaving Home

Ask him to please
never get a tattoo
involving the word
*Mom.*

Tell him you will always love him.

Remind him that beer is not one of the major food groups.

He will tell you that
you're the best mom in
the world and treat you
that way for the rest of
his life.

Hug him fiercely.

Tell him to text you,
email you, call you.
His choice.

Remember,
he'll be back.
He's hungry.

# Let him go.